Through The Mind Of Ah Young Lady

REMA FRAZIER HENDERSON, AUTHOR

Henderson, Rema Frazier
Through the Mind of Ah Young Lady

Copyright 2020 by KWE Publishing LLC
Original work by Rema Frazier Henderson

ISBN (paperback) 978-1-950306-01-5
ISBN (ebook) 978-1-950306-37-4

DEDICATIONS

This book is dedicated to my King, Mark Anthony, who protects and cares for his family. You are an awesome provider. You are there for your girls at all times, no matter what the need is. "You so good to me!"

This book is also dedicated to my two girls, Crista and Cristin, the most sweet and loving girls. You are experiencing similar things that I experienced in this book. I adore the both of you and it is a joy to see you both grow into adulthood. You three are the love of my life.

ACKNOWLEDGEMENTS

To God be the Glory for all of the things He has done. God is so awesome. When I look back over my life and see where He has brought me from, I can truly say that I am blessed. There were so many times I didn't know where my story would start and where it would end. Favor has been mine and my family's middle name. Thank you for favor, God.

It was a joy to meet the King of my life as a young lady. We have experienced so much together. Out of our unity, we have birthed two beautiful girls who look up to you as a true King. He's such a good provider and a caring man.

The Author gives a shout out to her three sisters and three brothers. We grew up close-knit. There were days when we loved each other, and there were days when we couldn't stand each other. But through it all, we learned to depend on each other through thick and thin. And last but not least, a shout out to Mamma, who is a strong sistah in Christ.

FOREWORD

We are excited to introduce to you our Mom. She is a woman who has always been there for us. She's never left us hanging for anything. She supports us in all that we set out to do. She's a mentor for us, she is a role model, and she motivates us on a daily basis through her inspirational texts! We can always depend on her to keep us "prayed up."

When our Mom opens her mouth and sings, I know that it is truly coming from God.

We are honored to have a chance to introduce you to our Mom and get to know her through this book.

Crista and Cristin

PREFACE

I'm excited and elated to be able to complete my second book project! After writing and publishing my first book, "Through The Eyes of Ah Gurl," I knew that a sequel was about to happen.

Some of the information in this book are things that I have seen and experienced through my eyes throughout the years. In the best interest of those whom I love dearly, there are no names mentioned except for my King. The information is captured through my thoughts through the "mind of ah young lady."

CHAPTER ONE

MY FIRST SCHOOL MUSIC EXPERIENCE

It was early one fall morning. It was the start of another school year. This was my very first year in high school. Freshman life, here I come! I arrived at the bus stop early that morning. I didn't want to have to run up the street with my cute first day of school outfit on. All of us kids on our street were dressed to perfection. At least we thought so anyways. We were wearing our nice new outfits with our matching brand new sneakers. Our backpacks and bookbags were brand spankin' new as well. There was nothing but smiles that morning. Even the neighborhood guy, who lived down the street who I had a crush on, was smiling. Normally he didn't talk much, but on that day he talked to everyone as they arrived at the bus stop.

The ride to school was a noisy one. Everybody talked about what their summer was like. Some of us were fortunate to go on a vacation out of the area, where some of us only went to visit family in other parts of the county. Some even were fortunate enough to go to amusement parks or to the beach. If you went to an amusement park or beach, you were considered one of the wealthier families in our little sub-division. Most of the families living in our sub-division didn't have a lot to splurge. Very few of them had both parents living in the household. If you had both parents living in the house, you were considered lucky. The majority of us only had our mammas living with us and a so-called daddy that would drop in a few times a week. We still considered ourselves lucky to have a house with a roof over our heads with running water and some food to eat. I don't even remember if I ate breakfast or not that morning, but I know one thing, that I was excited as heck to be going to high school.

We arrived at our high school bright and early that morning. The high school was really new, maybe 4 years old or so. The front of the school looked really small from the outside, but when we entered the school it seemed extremely big compared to our little old junior high school that had been there for years. Some of us had only been in the high school one time and that was during orientation day a few weeks earlier.

We already had our homeroom class number. We walked quickly down the long hallway to our homeroom classes. We didn't want to be late on the first day of school. While I was excited about my new clothes for the first day, I was also a little scared about starting the first day of my young high school life.

We all strutted down the hallway to our homerooms. All freshmen students were on the same hall so that was a good thing for us. That way we could all stay together. Each of us found our homerooms. As I entered my homeroom, I walked slowly through the door. There was no longer a smile on my face now. I saw the meanest looking homeroom teacher ever. As I walked in, she commanded me to have seat. Her voice was strong and confident. "Have a seat," she said. I quickly went to the first seat that I saw.

In junior high, I became the student that always wanted to fight other students. Not today. Soon after, the homeroom bell rang and she closed the big ole door to the room. She gave a few rules for her classroom and had us fill out some forms on the spot. She also gave us a package of documents to take home. The only document that I was really concerned about on that day was the one for the free lunch. My mamma always returned that one. There were five of us living with my mamma and she could not afford to buy lunch for us every school day.

Shortly after that, the first bell rang. It was so loud to me until it scared me. I actually jumped in my seat.

My first class period my freshman year in high school was Choir. I was really excited about that. The choir room was near the smoking area. I don't even know why but most of my friends hung out in the smoking area. Not so much to smoke, but to talk and sing and listen to music and to cuss and to skip school and whatever else they wanted to do.

I walked through the choir room door just as the late bell rang. As I walked in, I saw the prettiest little black teacher that I had ever seen in my entire life. She was my choir teacher. Through my eyes, she was perfect. This little lady was about 5 feet or so. She was wearing the brightest pink lipstick I had ever seen. It seemed as though her lips were always chapped. She had pretty, long, shoulder-length black hair. She was wearing the prettiest little two-piece pink tweed blend skirt suit, revealing her beautiful legs. She was wearing nude hosiery with the cutest little black heel pumps fitting perfectly on her size six and a half feet. Her suit was accessorized with the perfect pink blended matching jewelry.

Her style was sassy and classy. She was smart and pretty. Once I got to know her, I wanted so much to be just like her when I grew up. Her approach was definitely confident. She wasn't afraid of any of her students. Big or tall, short or small. She got you straight when she needed to. This little five-foot chick was no joke.

As I walked in going past her, she says to me "Take a seat please" in her sweet little voice. So I did of course. But in my mind I was thinking, "I can really get over on this lady. I can do just what I want to do in here." Was I ever wrong! After a few days, or perhaps a few weeks, of my chattering and playing around in class, she looks me dead in the eye and says "You will not act up in my class." All I knew was that I loved singing and I had come to realize that I loved choir. This was a place that I could come and release what I was thinking and release how I was feeling for the moment. So after a few weeks or perhaps months, I started acting up again. We were singing all different kinds of songs and I announced in the midst of the class by saying that "I don't like and don't want to sing them ugly songs." Well this little, pretty, well-put-together lady looked me in the eyes a second time and this time she says to me, "You will learn to like all kinds of music if you want to be in my class," and then she directed me to get out of her class.

I was devastated. I didn't know how in the world I was going get back in her choir class at that point. I had come to the realization that I truly had a love for music. Someone recommended that I go back and apologize to my choir teacher. I don't even know who it was. But I was very happy when my choir teacher accepted my apology and allowed me to come back to her choir class. Evidently, this little lady saw some type of potential in me. She took me under her wings and guided me throughout the next three years. As my music teacher had predicted, I did learn to love all types of music.

In retrospect, I felt like I was a bully towards my peers at times. Just plain old being mean! This awesome woman taught me how to be respectful to elders as well as to my schoolmates. I never knew what it meant to be grateful until I met this fabulous woman.

Throughout my high school years, I participated in talent shows and karaoke and church choirs and school choir concerts, just about anything that meant singing was involved. I started to have a really true love for music and being in the spotlight.

Because of this wonderful lady, I was accepted in the Regional Choir for the state of Virginia my Junior and Senior year of high school. I was also accepted into All District Choir my Senior year in high school, and I was the only Senior accepted from my high school. Because of the voice training that I received from this beautiful lady, I participated in a pageant, winning Second Runner Up and also winning the Talent Competition.

Through the mind of this young lady, my music teacher was like a mother figure. She gave me advice. She yelled at me when I needed it. She scolded me when I needed it and supported most of my high school singing events. She invested so much of her time in me. I am also sure that she invested some money in me as well that I didn't even know about. I am so grateful that I had a teacher like my music teacher back in those days to look up to. If this lady was alive today, she would be so proud of the lady that I have become.

♥

As I walked in the
choir room,
I saw the Prettiest
Little
Black teacher that
I had ever seen
in my entire life.

♥

CHAPTER TWO

MY FIRST WORK EXPERIENCES

Throughout my high school years, I worked several student co-op jobs. Co-op jobs were a collaboration between local companies and high schools. I didn't even know how much I was getting paid. I was just happy to have a job and to be able to make money.

My first job was working at a naval base where I was an assistant for a department chair. I worked in the evening around 2:30 until about 5 o'clock. My job consisted of Xeroxing and collating documents into a manual. This was one position that I seemed to have enjoyed.

My next job was working at Social Services as a file clerk. I would type and file case files for the social workers. This position caused me to mature very quickly because of the confidentiality of the materials handled. Sometimes I would read about someone I knew and it bothered me, but it taught me how to be responsible.

Luckily the programs provided transportation to and from the locations because we were not fortunate enough to have a car of our own.

In my eleventh-grade year, I was fortunate enough to get an after-school job with the electric company. My job was a meter-reader clerk. It taught me how to be responsible with paying my electric bill. If a meter reading was read a certain way, there was a possibility that the electricity could have been cut off. There were times when I would know an individual who was about to get their electricity turned off, and I would feel really bad for them.

I remember feeling the same way when I worked for the bank, and an individual that I knew had over-drafted their account. I remember having to call them to say, "Please come over as soon as possible to make a small deposit into your account!"

My senior year, I was fortunate to work on an army base in a reenlistment office. I loved that job. There were times that I was left alone to man the office. You think you are a big shot being left in charge of the office when you are seventeen! I would answer the phones and take messages, and greet the public. And I would do anything else that was needed. One thing I didn't do was to make coffee.

Fortunately, I stayed on after my school year ended and I graduated from high school. I was offered a summer job with the reenlistment office before going to college. Through the mind of this young lady, this job afforded me the opportunity to save some money for college.

♥

On that day,

I do believe that

God

Answered

Our Prayers!

♥

CHAPTER THREE

MY FIRST REAL FAITH

Have you ever been riding down the road and all of a sudden, you see something laying there that looks as though it's green? Well, one day, my cousin calls me and says, "Let's go and have lunch!" Have you ever had a cousin who never had money to go out? Well, I did. My cousin always wanted to go out to eat, but she never had a dime to pay for her food. At least, not back then.

On that particular day, we were riding down a little country road, talking, singing, and having fun. I had just gotten my little new/old Chevrolet Chevette, so I felt like I was sitting on top of the world. I could only afford to put $5 in my tank at a time. We didn't have very much money as young girls. So we had to make every penny count.

So we decided to go to have a bite to eat. Back in those days, there weren't very many places that we could go. There was probably McDonald's, Hardees, Dairy Queen, Long John Silver's, Pierce's BBQ, and Sal's Pizza. We truly had to decided what we could afford to eat.

On that day, I do believe that God answered our prayers. As we rode down that little crooked road, it seems as though the money fell from the sky. It was green and it was crumpled up. I'm sure that several cars had gone by and not even have noticed it. There was several cars ahead of me, and there were several cars behind me.

All of a sudden, I stopped in the middle of the road, and I asked my cousin, "Did you see that?" And she answered me, "What?" I told her, "That looks like money!" And she says, "Who would put money in the road?"

I was sure I saw money so I got out of the car. Not to mention that I held up all the traffic! I opened my door quickly. I did remember to put the car in park! And I slowly walked in front of the car. I looked down and there it was.

Crumpled up dollar bills! I don't even remember how much it was but I do know that it was enough to feed the both of us.

Through the minds of these young ladies, we truly believed that this money fell from the sky. And this was truly a blessing from God. From that point forward, my faith was so strong even as a young lady.

♥

Money fell from the sky

For my cousin

And I!

♥

CHAPTER FOUR

THE COUSINS STORY

In my teenage years, my cousins were like my sisters and brothers. My two boy cousins lost their mom at an early age. So the oldest one of them ended up moving in with my aunt and the youngest one ended up living with us. He was like my very own big brother.

He could make me do all kinds of bad things, like fight the kids down the road! He would get me to errands for him. "Go in the kitchen and get me some water!" and things like that.

I wasn't all that close to the older brother. I don't even know why. He would always go down the road. He was older than we were and felt like he didn't want to play with us kids.

So my other cousins also lost their mom when they were very young. They were like my sisters. In fact, everybody thought that we were sisters, especially the older one. She had the same complexion as I did. The thing that really made us look like sisters was that we had the big eyes alike. Every Sunday, we would all gather at my grandmother's house. My grandmother made the best homemade rolls. So, when we got home from church on Sunday, she would always have hot rolls and chicken ready for us grandchildren. We would all go out and play kickball and tag. Towards the evening, we would all gather in my grandmother's house and sing. Even the older ones, who wouldn't play with us, would sing with us.

Pretty much all of the grandchildren could sing, with the exception of my cousin that lived with my aunt. But he always loved singing and taking the lead. For instance, he took over the song, "Oh Happy Day!" His younger brother was quiet. He didn't really care for being seen or singing out loud.

My other aunt had one daughter that lived with our great aunt in another town. She also had three boys. The youngest boy was like our little adopted brother. He always tried to make us do what he wanted us to do. For instance, he wanted to always come to our house and play when we had to do chores. The middle and the older son only came over when they wanted something to borrow.

My aunt that lived down the road had older children. They were too old for me to play with or hang out with. The only time they would want to bother with us was when they wanted us to babysit their children. For some reason, they never wanted to pay us for babysitting, even for the times that the kids spent the night with us. Now ain't that something?

My other aunt was the bossy one. She had one much older daughter and a daughter a year older than me. She had two sons. One was a year younger than me, and another was three years younger than me. She would always bring her kids to my grandma's house. All except for the oldest daughter, because she was much older than we were and could stay by herself. This aunt always wanted her kids to eat up all of our snacks and food. Of course, we would fight about whose food belonged to who. My mama bought most of the food in the house, which wasn't a whole lot for all of us.

So my uncle's kids, they were never close to us in our younger days, although they lived just down the road. I'm not even sure why. We all went to school together, and I didn't even know that they were really my cousins for a good while. Every so often, they would come up to my grandmother's house and spend a few hours.

My great-uncle's grandkids that lived next door to my grandma were really close to us. We would hang out at their house, sing and play board games, and things like that.

Most of us girl cousins sang in the choir and played on the softball team. There were days when we would go play softball and then leave there, half-dirty, and go sing for the evening revival. We wouldn't have time to take a shower or anything. We would just brush our hair up, wash our faces, put on some lipstick, dress up, and go and sing for revivals! These were two things that we loved doing: singing and playing softball.

One of my older cousins was our coach for the girls' softball team. Our team was one of the better teams in the county. At least, I thought we were. My cousin played first base, my younger sister played second base, and I was one of the best shortstop players (and that's not really true!). My cousin that looked like me played third base. Now, she was really good! And she could really sing, also. A lady outside of the family played catcher and our coach's wife was the pitcher. My two sister-cousins played right field and left field. And my cousin that looked like me, her sister was bad in center field!

So the boy cousins were great at playing softball and singing as well. That was like a family trait. I really think it was like a neighborhood thing that most of us did.

♥

I loved my cousins
As though they were
My sisters
And brothers.

♥

CHAPTER FIVE

MY FIRST BOYFRIEND

It was the last semester in high school my senior year. I met this young man through a friend. I would see him at parties, and I thought he was a really nice young man with a beautiful smile. So we met at a couple of parties and decided to go out. Neither one of us had a car. His cousin transported us everywhere. We went out to dinner with his cousin and his friend.

It always seemed like we would go to his aunt's house just to hang out. This young man loved his aunt and his grandma. We would just talk and watch TV. Sometimes until we would fall asleep! So back in those days, your parents didn't worry about where you were. Sometimes I would wait until his cousin came home to take me home the next morning.

So we officially started dating. And I asked if he would be my date for my senior prom. He was also a senior at another school. So he accepted.

And we went to my senior prom together. We both decided to wear beige with white accessories.

On the night of the prom, we met at my house to go out. We double dated with my brother and his date. My brother was driving us and I don't even remember whose car he had. I remember it being a big car. We stayed out half of the night after the prom riding around, talking, having fun, and smooching. My brother and his date dropped me off early the next morning.

We dated for the rest of the semester. I was accepted at college in another state and he was accepted at a college in the state that we lived in. After he learned that I was accepted at an out-of-state college, he decides he wants to go to the same college that I'm accepted at. That was a bad decision.

When you're in college with your so-called boyfriend, you have no freedom. Everywhere I went, he wanted to hang with me. That was getting old real soon!

But this is what he decided to do. After the first semester, he decided to go into the military. We hung in there as boyfriend and girlfriend for some months. And he gave me an engagement ring!

After about a month or so, we talked and I found out that he was going overseas. We officially decided at that point we would no longer be boyfriend and girlfriend. So in the mind of this young lady, I'm thinking, "So, why did he give me a ring?" Several months later, we spoke again. So at that point, it was totally over! He notified me and said that he was going to be stationed overseas. Before he left, he wanted to come and pick up the ring that he had given me. I thought that was really funny. You don't give somebody a gift and take it back! I had different thoughts about him. That really made me think badly about him at that point.

We agreed that he would come to my house to pick up the ring. So that day, it was a warm, sunny day. And we chatted for a few minutes. He still acted like he was in love with me. And of course, I still cared about him, but not like I did before. After giving him his ring, we gave each other a friendly hug, and he left my house.

When I returned to college second semester, I was all by myself. Talk about having a good time! I had so much fun. I did my schoolwork, but I was a party girl, too!

I didn't hear of my first boyfriend for several years. I saw his family member and they told me that he was still in the military.

♥

You don't give someone a gift and then take it back!

♥

CHAPTER SIX

THE FIRST YEAR OF COLLEGE AWAY FROM HOME

As the time approached and the day arrived for me to load up my stuff and take the long ride to a place that I had never seen, this young lady was so afraid to step out and venture out. A few days prior to my leaving for this tremendous adventure, I was informed that another girl from my high school was going to the same college as I was. That made me feel a whole lot better.

The other young girl had not experienced much outside of the state of Virginia, let alone the town that we grew up in, no more than I had. What she did know was that she was ready to make that move as well. I was told that she had waited a year before going to college. Scared and excited at the same time, we took that long two hour ride to another state. When we arrived, there were people everywhere. Going in buildings, coming out of buildings. Carrying boxes and clothes. Hugging each other good bye. A few cries every now and then.

We found the dorm that we were going to be living in. It was one of the better and bigger dorms on campus. I guess it does pay off to apply late. We both signed in and received our dorm room keys. While we were in the same building and on the same floor, we were in different rooms. We headed up the steps to our rooms all the way on the third floor. There were not elevators back in those days. We had to take the steps for everything. We were exhausted every day.

We got to my dorm room first. My friend proceeded down the hall to her room. To my surprise as I opened the dorm room door, I was in for the shock of my life. My roommate was an albino girl from Africa. She was snow white in color in her face. Her hair was blond-orange in these little squiggly round circles all over her head. I almost fainted. And that is no lie. She scared me to death! I had never seen anyone like this ever in my life.

Back in those days, we didn't understand about a person having a condition like that. This was totally new to my world.

I walked in the room slowly with my Mama and my Daddy walking behind me. I put my luggage down. The room had this weird smell and it was freezing cold! I don't even remember speaking to the girl. And I don't even remember her speaking to me. I couldn't even tell you to this day what her name was. All I know is that someone had told me that she was from Africa. So we left the room immediately. Shortly after that, they left to go home. They didn't even stay long enough to see what was going to happen.

After they left, I went downstairs to the office to request another room. There was absolutely no way that I was going to stay in that room that night. I was told that I couldn't switch rooms for a week. I was devastated. So I went to find the girl that was from my hometown. Her room was down the hall from mine. I knocked on the door hard. So she came to the door and opened it, and I started telling my story about my roommate. Her roommate was a normal-looking girl like we were. And she was very friendly. So I got to telling her more about my roommate, and that's when I asked, "Can I sleep in your room for a week?" And she was like, "We only have two beds!" And that's when I said, "I guess I'm going to have to sleep at the foot of your bed!" I didn't even know her like that. She wasn't too excited about it but she said, "I guess so."

So I went to get some of my stuff. And my stuff had already started to smell like the room! I didn't even explain to the girl I was staying in another room or anything! I just never came back to the room unless I needed to.

After about a week, I was able to get another room. So I moved all of my stuff to my new room. When I opened the door to my new room, I saw a girl that looked more like me but she was very harsh. She did speak to me. And we started talking about where we were from. She was from the Islands. That seemed so far from home to me. She had already been on campus for a week or so before I got there. So she seemed very lonely. She seemed to be a very nice person. After getting to know her for a while, I found out that she was not a happy person. She was grumpy all the time. That was the experience of my first year in college. Through the mind of a young lady, I learned a lot of lessons about life that particular year.

♥

She was Snow White
In color,
Her hair was orange.
I almost fainted when
I saw her!

♥

CHAPTER SEVEN

THE SECOND YEAR: FALLING IN LOVE

After a great summer at home, it was time for me to return to college to start another chapter in my life, my second year of college. I was a pro at this! I knew just what to do. I got my classes registered and went to the bookstore to get my books. And I saw the most handsome guy that I had ever seen!

He was tall, slim, and poised. His style of dressing was awesome! He had on nice jeans with a very nice shirt with a blazer. His shoes were so shined and neat. He wore a belt in his jeans matching the shoes, which is a plus for me. He suave-ayed around the bookstore with this smile that could outshine the sun! He had the prettiest white teeth and his goatee was groomed to perfection. His hair was freshly cut. I overheard him speak to a friend. When he spoke, his voice was a soft baritone. That was like music to my ears!

When I got back to my dorm, I got the opportunity to meet my second-year roommate in college. She was short, cute, dressed nicely, and really loud. Everything she talked about, she spoke loudly. But she was an extremely nice person from what I could see. So we decided to go together to the cafeteria along with another girl that came from the same high school that she did.

As we walked through the line to get our food, there were several guys standing around. We casually spoke and what to my surprise was Mr. Gorgeous himself! So I started feeling a little flirty. I could tell he had his eyes on me. I still didn't get to formally meet him.

So several days went on. On that Saturday, there was a campus party. There was music playing, lots of people gathered. And as my roommate and I walked in, there he was again. He was standing there with several guys. They were all nicely dressed guys. This time, he was really dressed. Dress pants, blazer, collared shirt, and the shiniest shoes that I'd ever seen. He came up to me and asked me to dance. And I accepted. That was back in the day when I knew that I could dance.

We began to dance, and I found out that he could really dance, too! I discovered that all of the guys from the D.C. area were really great dancers. They knew every dance there was. On top of that, they were really cool, really smart guys. I enjoyed hanging out with them.

He asked to walk me to my dorm. That was the most wonderful feeling. He was such a gentleman. I don't think we kissed on the first night. I believe we hugged instead.

All night, all I could think of was this really good-looking guy! I couldn't wait until the next morning when I could run into him, hoping that he would want to walk me to class.

The next day, I didn't see him until dinnertime. That made me think he was really into his schoolwork. So we decided to hang out at the library, and then we started really spending time together. We decided that we were boyfriend and girlfriend. So we spent quality time together. During that time, the song, "The Second Time Around" was out. And I felt like he was my second time around.

♥

He was tall, slim, and Poised. His style of dressing was Awesome!

♥

CHAPTER EIGHT

THE FIRST BLACK BANK CLERK

When I worked for the bank, I was the first black bank clerk ever hired there as far as I'm aware. I remember the first day walking through those doors for my interview, I was so scared. I don't even remember getting the call for the interview. But I know somehow it did. I remember it was early in the morning, but I'm not a really early morning girl, but I am a people person. So I had this big smile on my face when I walked in. I saw nothing that looked like me.

I was raised to be very polite and cordial to people so I spoke. I had to practice my confidence and to have courage. I had on my cute little two-piece suit. Because I was little then – at least I thought I was. And it was fitting so well. I had on a black suit with black heels. And I had on makeup on and my lipstick. We couldn't afford a lot of fancy stuff but I had on the "bestest." That's better than the best – that I had!

I introduced myself to the bank manager. And then he introduced me to other members of the bank. At that point, I kind of knew I had the job. But I was really scared because I had never worked around lots of money like that. But he made me feel really comfortable.

A lady joined us with the man. At that time, I was about to go into my second year of college so we talked about my education, the things I liked, hobbies, and things like that. Another thing that drew them to me was that I was in the local pageant my senior year of high school. They were very impressed with that! They were also impressed that a little country girl went to school in another state. They just didn't know that I hadn't been to any other place in the world! But I carried it well. You know how you "fake it till you make it?" That's exactly what I had to do.

After my interview, I was offered the position, They told me the position was 5 days a week. I was thinking, I had never worked anywhere five days a week. I wasn't used to having to be at work on time and to get there on my own. So I was really thinking about, "How am I going to get to work every day, Monday through Friday?" Some of the older people in my neighborhood didn't have the privilege to be off on weekends and holidays!

I had to catch the public bus to work; therefore, I had to leave earlier than I would have if I had a car. My mom did not drive, and my other relatives were not able to transport me to work. There was one neighbor that was so kind. He would always offer me a ride to work. And he was one of the most respectful men that I knew back in those days.

After about a month, the bank manager came to me and asked if I had transportation, and asked if I wanted to finance a car through the bank. I didn't even know how to look for a car! But then, we found this little old, 1979, grey Chervrolet Chevette down the street from my grandmother's house. And we took a test drive. I wasn't that great of a driver!

The bank financed my first car. I didn't even know how much it cost. It might have been $3,000 which back then was a lot. My payment was about $100 a month. I loved that little grey Chevette! I kept it until the day I left to go to go overseas. And then I have it to a relative.

I no longer needed to catch the bus or get a ride for work. It felt so good to have my own transportation.

After working at the bank for several months, I learned that there was another girl who competed in the local pageant. She was a student at a nearby college. I felt like I was more intelligent being in the company of people like that.

When I first started off, I was hired as a bank teller. I only did that just to learn how to do it if I had to. But my real job was as an accounts clerk where I would open and close the accounts. There were days when I did some applications for a loan as well.

I only worked in the bank for a little over a year. I started off for the summer, and then went back to school. After graduating from a junior college, I was hired as a permanent employee where I stayed until I got married.

♥

It was an honor
To have been hired
As the very first black
Bank clerk at the
Banking
Establishment.

♥

CHAPTER NINE

THE FIRST FAMILY MEMBER TO GRADUATE FROM COLLEGE AND TO LIVE ON CAMPUS

It had been two long years at college, and the day had arrived when it was time for me to graduate! Before I could finish, I had to take one accounting class at William & Mary in the fall to get the credits I needed to graduate the next spring. After the class was completed, the credits were transferred back to and approved by the college.

When I got the notification that everything was approved, I became extremely excited! I leaped in the air and I screamed. You would have thought that I was getting a PhD!

I received the dates and times of graduation and other events surrounding this happy day. I ordered my cap and gown so I could walk in the spring graduation. It was a wonderful feeling.

My family members were invited to the ceremony. Unfortunately, only my Momma and my Daddy and a few other family members attended because of the distance. In addition, some of them had to work. Through the mind of this young lady, the most important person attending was my King, my boyfriend. He was so supportive of me graduating and doing big things in life.

♥

When I got the
Notification that

everything

Was accepted,

I was so

Excited!

♥

CHAPTER TEN

THE DAY I MET MY KING

Sometimes, my friends and I would go out clubbing, dancing, and having fun! We would dress up in the cutest outfits and I would pick them up. Being that I was the only one who had a car! I was driving my grey Chevrolet Chevette that I had only had for no more than a year. We would often head to Fort Eustis. This was one of the hottest spots during that time! All of the young ladies that I knew of would go there to party and to meet a handsome, young man.

I had this one girlfriend that would always refuse to go. She said that her grandmama said, "Fort Eustis ain't no place for no decent young girl!" But on one particular night, I did talk her into going. She was so horrified because her grandmama had brainwashed her about going to a military base! Well, when we got there, she was afraid to go in. And we weren't about to take her all the way back home. So she just sat in the car the whole night! But she really didn't mind because she was convinced she wasn't going in.

On another cool, fall night, some friends and I decided we were going to go out clubbing again at Fort Eustis. On this particular night, we had gone out and bought new outfits to wear and we left home about 9 o'clock. When we got there, the club was packed. Parking was awful! We had to drive around several times before we could find a parking spot.

The club was filled with familiar faces. I ran into some girls I knew from my hometown. There were guys that I had seen before but didn't know much about them. As I was on the dance floor dancing, I spotted this handsome, slim, young man! He was sitting there all alone. I guess we caught eye contact because the next song that came on, he asked me to dance. He was trying to be all cool with his dance, not knowing that he really couldn't dance at all! Throughout the entire song, he did nothing but a two-step.

He tried to talk to me but the music was so loud I could barely hear him. So I sort of played him off. I went to sit with my girls and I started talking about how good-looking he was.

The next song came on, and he asked me to dance again, but this time, we danced a little further away from the speakers so we could talk a bit. So he asked me my name. And I told him, of course. And so I asked him his name, and he told me. It seemed as though we danced the entire night together.

Towards the end of the night, he asked me for my phone number, and I refused to give it to him. But then he gave me his. That was a smart move on his part. So we departed that night and gave our goodbyes.

The next day, I remembered the number in my purse. And I was contemplating giving him a call. I decided not to for that day. I'm like, "No, I won't call him. I'll let him wait a few days." Back in those days, they lived in the barracks and they didn't have personal phones. So I had to call the hall phone shared by everyone on the floor.

After about two days, I decided to call the number. And the military person on duty answered the phone. When I asked for his name, the duty person yelled out his name down the hall! After about two minutes, I heard this deep voice answer, "Hello?"

I got so nervous and I didn't even know what to say! I said, "Hello, how are you?" or something like that. He came back with, "I'm fine." Our sentences were two to three words. We didn't know what to say to each other.

He did ask me if I was coming to the club that following weekend. And I did answer, "Maybe." But of course, I had to round up two of my closest girls who would always ride with me to Fort Eustis. We never did invite my friend back who sat in the car!

So we did go out that following Friday to Fort Eustis. We arrived fairly early this time because

Fridays were "Ladies Night" where we got in half price. The line was long, coming out the door. And it was a chilly night. Once we got in the club, we found a seat and sat there for a while before we danced. You have to observe first!

My girlfriends went on and got a drink. I was always the designated driver because I didn't drink. And then here comes this handsome young man, who comes up to the table and speaks. And of course, I spoke back with my gorgeous face!

He asked me if I wanted something to drink. And then I said, "Yes, I'll take a Coke." I told him that I didn't drink. I think he was drinking something like a rum and Coke.

We hung out and danced and talked the whole night! I found out that he didn't have a car at that time. He walked from the barracks to get to the club. When the night was over, I didn't even offer him a ride back to the barracks. I just let him walk.

The next day, he wanted to come and visit me. So he caught the Greyhound bus to see me. I was so impressed by that. I picked him up at the bus station. I wasn't about to go to Fort Eustis and pick him up and bring him back to my house because I didn't know a lot about the area at the time.

♥

She said that

Her grandmama said,

"Fort Eustis

Ain't no place

For no decent young

girl!"

♥

CHAPTER ELEVEN

THE WEDDING DAY OF A LIFETIME

THE BEGINNING OF A DREAM

Fall was about to approach. It was nice and cool outside, a late August evening. Me and my girls decided we wanted to take a ride. We ended up stopping in at Fort Eustis.

I had already spoken with my King earlier in the afternoon and I talked about perhaps coming to the club that night. We didn't decide to meet or anything, and he didn't say he was coming. But who shows up? My little handsome man was there!

We danced and we danced most of the night. We mingled with my girls at the same time. It was a great night. When the club was about to close, I couldn't hang out with him any longer that night. I had the girls with me and we had to go home. And that was in 30 minutes!

By then, this handsome young man owned a car. So the next day, he decided to come and visit. We went to the park and ate dinner. We hung out all evening. By then, he was starting to meet some of my family members.

One of my closest aunts lived up the street from us so I took him to meet her. This particular aunt didn't like anybody! But she liked him! She just took to him so easily. And that was a great thing.

We stayed at her house a while, sat, and had a few things to eat while we talked. The night was starting to get pretty late. He left to go back to Fort Eustis because he lived on base.

By now, I've been starting to know him close to a month. We were starting to do more things together. So I asked him to come to church with me, because my family is big on going to church. And I was very active in my church choir. He agreed with me and decided to go. For me, that was a big plus.

After that, for several months, he started going to church with me. We would go to family events together. We were getting closer and closer at that time.

Several more months passed. We were at the point where we were showing more affection to each other. He was a true gentleman, and he would do things like hold the door for me and give me flowers and beautiful gifts. We started going to the movies together. We were going out more steadily, just the two of us.

Around December time frame, he finds out he has orders to go to overseas. And he decides he does want to leave his Rema behind. It had only been eight months by then. He mentioned getting married, and I thought it was a little too soon. But he did not. I had never been overseas before, let alone any further than the state of New York. This was a big thing for me.

A month or so had gone by. Then I discovered we were really getting close in our relationship. I really had to think about, did I really want to lose him by having him go overseas alone, or consider marrying him? And then another thing that came to mind was, did I really love him? I wasn't sure that maybe I just didn't want to lose him.

While sitting out at a park, he unofficially proposed to me. He didn't get down on one knee and say, Will you marry me? None of that. We were just talking. I remember mentioning it to my mom and he mentioned it to my daddy. My dad didn't comment one way or the other about my decision but he was very supportive.

So we decided to go on and get married. We got married in March of 1982. I decided to marry him because I didn't want to lose him and I knew that he was an extremely good man.

We ended up having a fairly big wedding. I asked five of my close friends to be my bridesmaids and then asked one of my younger sisters to be my maid of honor. I didn't have a matron of honor at the time because none of my friends were married. Each of my girls got their own dresses made. Back in those days, everything was pretty much made! I provided the pattern and the material, and they go their own seamstress to make their dresses. The girls that went clubbing with me were not even a part of the wedding. My family members did all my catering for the wedding. My father's friend was our bartender. A friend of mine was our DJ. And a friend of mine did all my flowers. My pastor officiated the wedding. This pastor was like a father to a lot of us growing up in our church. The groomsmen consisted of a couple of my fiancé's friends, my brother, and one of my very close male friends that I graduated with from high school. And to this day, he is still one of my really close friends. It was exciting to have him in my wedding because his brother was a professional football player. The guys wore white tuxedos. And my King wore a white tuxedo with tails!

The most important thing about my wedding was my white dress. It was loaned to me by a friend that I worked with in the bank. It had a beautiful train and it was tailor-made with rhinestones.

And my cousin sang at my wedding as a soloist. She sung one of my favorite songs that I still love to this very day, "Endless Love". Her accompanist was a very close friend of mine for years.

He left to go overseas in April. He had to go by himself first as he received orders before we were married. One month later, he made sure that I was there. He had found an apartment for us prior to me coming over.

That was my very first time flying, and I had to fly alone to another country! My flight was wonderful considering it was my first time. I flew to New York to JFK. It was like culture shock for me considering the size of JFK! When I got there, it was like a dream because there were so many people. But I made it to my connection flight, and it was such a relief once I got on the plane.

Flying for me was so amazing because as I sat on the seat as we took off, I wondered, How did this plane go up in the air like this and go through the clouds? I think that was my very first time believing in God! For a 23 year old girl who had never been outside of the United States, this was truly amazing!

This eight hour ride was so fabulous! I felt like I was being pampered and catered to. I remember receiving dinner and snacks and drinks and watching movies the entire long, eight hour flight.

♥

For a 23 year old girl

Who had never been

Outside of the United

States,

Flying was

Truly amazing!

♥

CONCLUSION

In conclusion, I hope you've enjoyed these stories captured and written through the mind of ah young lady. I've certainly enjoyed taking the time to share certain portions of my life as a young lady with you. I pray these stories will be an inspiration for you!

BeBlessed Y'all!

LuvyLuv!

Rema